Close more contracts

~ with ~

HOSPITALITYCOPYWRITING

Jeremiah Magone

Consulting Copywriter

5007 Milton St.

San Diego, CA 92110

jeremiah@hospitalitycopywriting.com

(619) 445 – 4319

1

Hospitality B2B Copywriting Services Packet

Nurture relationships – overcome buying objections – and close more deals!

NURTURE RELATIONSHIPS

Follow-up is essential for building B2B relationships. Businesses that understand that fact lower their marketing expense, enjoy more repeat business and larger contracts. Those that don't – fail.

OVERCOME BUYING OBJECTIONS

Hotel owners are too busy to talk and GMs hate dealing with sales calls. That's why you need sales materials that can keep your leads hot and overcome buying objections over the span of several months.

CLOSE MORE DEALS

An effective sales funnel takes the work out of nurturing leads, guarantees your business a constant stream of pre-sold prospects and allows you to invest your time and energy where it belongs – closing more deals.

Unlock your company's revenue potential with secrets

from the only copywriting service specializing in hospitality B2B sales.

As far as I can find on Google, this is it.

HospitalityCopywriting.com

"It's hard to find a copywriter who can be successful with business-to-business, high-tech accounts," a prospect told me over the phone today, "especially in the hospitality industry, where there's so much competition for decision makers' time."

Do you have that same problem?

If so, please take some time to look over my copywriting service packet. In it, you'll see: who I work for, what I can do for you and how we can work together.

You get my client and professional experience list… client testimonials … a short bio … samples of my B2B and B2C work in the hospitality industry… a fee schedule listing what I charge for ads, brochures, and other assignments … sample content marketing articles… and an example of a branding platform that I use call the Key Copy Platform.

From experience I've learned that the best time to evaluate a copywriting service is before you need them… not when a deadline comes crashing around the corner.

In fact, that's the worst time to try to gage anyone's abilities and professionalism...

So whether you have an immediate project, a future need, or are just curious to learn about what's working in hospitality B2B sales these days, I urge you to send a contact request so we can set up a call.

4

Why not fill out this online RFP form today?

http://eepurl.com/cbgL2j

Or just pick up the phone and give me a call! That way we can have a short conversation… share a few ideas for selling your products and services… and see if we're a good fit.
Looking forward to speaking with you.

Sincerely,

Jeremiah

Jeremiah Magone

P.S. Don't bet the success of your campaign on someone you've never even talked to! Call me today at (619) 445 – 4319. There's no charge for a cost estimate. And no obligation to buy.

"For me, whatever project we undertake together, it's my mission to find new ways to help your business connect. That means successful promotions, of course. But it also means giving you a way leverage those promotions in a variety of ways for even bigger returns on your investment in the future."

– Jeremiah Magone

➢ See my [services page](#) and give your business the ***lead nurturing*** advantage. P. 8

Persuasive web copy

For your promotions to be successful on the web, they have to be energetic, deeply personal, and tirelessly lead your readers forward->forward->forward->. That's what *"Click-Forward Content"™* is all about.

It's compelling. It's urgent. And it has one undeniable conclusion.

That's the only way you can cut through all the competition in the busy B2B world these days... and that's the only way you can build the traction you need for successful contract negotiations.

➢ Please see my [samples page](#) for proof of this persuasive writing style. P. 19

> "His passion for his work, his creative mind, original thinking, and his ability to problem solve are echoed by his talent with the written word."
>
> Laura Hill, Coronado School of Arts Director.

B2B content marketing

My business experience has taught me that promotional development IS product development. Nowhere is this more important than in the tourism industry. That's because every one of your customers wants to be able to experience the benefits of your product or service before they sign up. That's why, as a copywriter, my entire focus is on helping you leverage your product development with your marketing plan so we can create the right appeal and, along with it, the biggest return on your investment. It doesn't make any sense to have a superior product or price if you aren't telling people about it, in a way they can emotionally connect with.

➢ Please see my [clients and experiences page](#) for examples of how I've helped other businesses. P. 14

6

Give your business a new sales funnel

Many marketers don't realize how hard it is for hotel businesses to find what they're looking for in all the noise. So, instead of actively forging connections that lead to sales, they spend all their time providing tons of information on their products and services. It seems that they only know how to talk about themselves.

To cut through the noise, your marketing message needs to do something decidedly different. It needs to speak directly to your prospects in their own language. It needs to reach out to them and show that you understand their needs, wants and desires. That's the only way you're going to create a real connection.

> "The day that I returned to the art gallery after leaving Jeremiah by himself so that I could run some errands and found 6... 7... 8 art pieces tagged and paid for, I knew that I had hired the right salesman for the job."
>
> Glen McNary,
> The Coronado
> Art Gallery

This is where a tailored sales funnel strategy can give you a huge advantage over your competition.

Altogether, this personal approach helps your business:

1. Get attention – Driving traffic to your site in multiple ways.

2. Build trust – By showing that you're the likable subject matter expert.

3. Convert – Drive sales by staying in front of your prospects on a regular basis, while continually showing them how your products or services will change their lives for the better... all with an irresistible offer.

4. Deliver satisfaction – Because by giving your customers a sense of support and confidence through your website, you build loyalty. And that lets you grow your business.

If you're curious to learn exactly how I can add these 4 elements to your current promotional materials, just give me a call and ask for one of my "Copy Critiques". It's a fast and inexpensive way to try my services without jumping into a full-fledged campaign. And it'll give you a clear picture of how I would approach your specific business.

Also, for those interested in branding, please see my Key Copy Platform sample, P. 36

Lessons I learned from promoting the launch of Revolution Magazine

 I know how important it is for everything in your campaign to come together in one stunning and seamless presentation. I've learned this by doing numerous art shows of my own, opening businesses, publishing, and most notably when I helped with the national launch of the electronica magazine, "Revolution", featuring Madonna. There can't be any mistake when you're doing big things. That's why I make sure that, whether you're coordinating a multi-segment email campaign or working to stay in front of your in-house list, the work you receive for me will be top notch, every time.

> ➤ Please see my **system used page** to understand the writing influences and techniques that I bring to your promotions. P. 24

"Mr. Jeremiah Magone possesses fine character traits. He has always pursued his own path, excelled in what he set out to do, and carried through on assigned tasks."

Tom Yamamoto, Owner of Tom's language school.

A team of experts on your side

 I go the extra mile to make sure your promotion is the best it can be by working closely with a group of professional copywriters and supporting editors. Since 2013, our group has been meeting weekly to test new techniques for increasing open rates, sharing the latest trends in marketing, and continually critique each other's work in an effort to make every one of your promotions as powerful and revenue producing as possible.

That's why, when you work with me, you'll know that you're receiving, not only the smoothest, most flawless copy possible, but also – my very best work to date.

> ➤ Please see my **pricing page** for rates, terms and FAQs. P. 9

"Jeremiah's focus on delivering quality content for our clients is 2nd to none. He's the best copywriter we've ever worked with."

Nicholas Slettengren,

Partner,

Power Digital Marketing.

Promotions that you can use for years to come

It's my aim to learn everything I can about your company, competition and your specific demographic market before I ever sit down to write. It's a lot of work, but I do it for a reason. I know that I'll only succeed in my promotion if you succeed. And that means making you more money from your marketing than you've ever seen before. This is my long term goal - because if I can do that, I know that we'll be working together for years to come. After all, that's a win-win situation for everyone.

➢ Please see my **biography page** to learn a little about the personality that I bring to your promotions. P. 27

Give me a call to talk about your next campaign… It doesn't cost you anything, and it may even help clarify your current marketing situation. Let me show you how persuasive copy can help make your business as profitable as it can be.

Sincerely,

Jeremiah Magone

Consulting copywriter

Hospitality Copywriting.com

Proud member of:

 HospitalityCopywriting.com

Services page

Nurture relationships – overcome buying objections – and close more deals!

Research <u>confirms</u> the age-old adage:

Repeat Business Is The Best Business.

You can grow your sales volume by **20%...**

Score **47%** larger purchases…

Cut your marketing budget by **1/3**…

> As reported by DemandGen report, The Annuitas Group and Forrester Research, respectively.

All by deciding to focus on the customers you already know.

Just ask yourself, **as an owner**, do you want to close one sale on one occasion or do you want spend a little extra effort to make sure that business comes back to you again and again?

It's not a very tough choice… Which is why I take the approach of *lead nurturing* in every step of your promotions. For example:

Of course I can...   **But we can also!**

Write direct response letters, brochures and other marketing materials.

- Send out a teaser auto-responder series to personally invite your customer base to check in on these new materials and offers.

close **more** contracts

HospitalityCopywriting.com

Write your high impact sales pages to turn interested visitors into ready buyers, today!	• Make the headlines, big idea and your central promise just the right size to be converted into tweets. I'll even add a convenient button…
Give you a Video Sales Letter that works as well as any real life sales representative.	• Publish the content of that letter as an e-book. This gives you 10 pages of Google search results… and it provides a great opt-in piece.
Give you SEO friendly articles that will help you connect with your readers needs.	• Use the research that I do to write those articles as a chance to reach out to past customers to listen to them and show how much you care.
Write e-newsletters that establish you as an expert that people know, like and trust.	• Offer to exchange links with your readership at the bottom of your newsletter. Do some mini advertising for you community and watch it pay off!

Get in touch with me at HospitalityCopywriting.com today and let me show you the results that *lead nurturing* can bring to your business.

HospitalityCopywriting.com

Pricing page

This pricing sheet reflects estimates for various projects and is only valid for 90 days after receipt. For a complete price prospectus, please get in touch with me directly and I'll be happy to provide you with a tailored marketing plan to meet your business goals.

Service description	Fees
Video Sales Letter – 3 minutes.	$675 – $2,000 + 5% commission
Sales Letter	$1,200 - $5,050 + 5% commission
Website - home page	$1,500 - $2,700
Website - other pages	$750 - $975/page
Landing page	$1,550 - $2,350
Order device	$925 - $1,375
Microsite	$2,350 - $5,000
E-newsletter set up	$2,600
E-newsletter monthly	$650
Online ad	$500 - $700
Email, long copy – series of 5	$1,900 - $2,500 + 5% commission
Email, short copy – series of 5	$1,175 - $1,700 + 5¢ per click
Email, lead generation – 7	$1,100 - $1,500 + 2¢ per click
Direct mail package - mail order	$4,850 - $6,400 + 5¢ per mailing
Side-by-side ad package - house list	$1,500 - $3,600 + 5¢ per mailing
Membership renewal series	$1,350 - $2,100/letter
Self-mailer	$1,850 - $3,950
Postcard or double postcard	$750 - $1,125 + 2¢ per mailing
Brochure – 3 fold	$855 - $1,350
Print ads	$850 - $2,600
Newsletter	$500 - $1,100/mailing

HospitalityCopywriting.com

Feature story	$950 – $1,350
White paper	$3,100 - $3,800
Case Study	$1,600 - $1,850
Japanese / Spanish SEO meta text	$150 - $200/ page
Japanese / Chinese translations	$150/page
Spanish translations	$75/ page
Japanese / Chinese lead generation tweets – (20)	$375
Spanish lead generation tweets – (20)	$200
Copy critique	$380 - $940
SEO friendly articles	$850 - $1,100
Blog post	$235 - $500
Press Release (1-2 pages)	$350 - $700

*Prices only valid until Feb, 2017

Description of online copywriting services

Video Sales Letter —$575 – $1,900 + 5% commission

A long-copy sales letter in video form with pictures, music and native level narration, designed to sell a product or secure a reservation – ideal for hotels, malls, tourism boards, local shops and high-end tour programs. The equivalent of a 3 to 5-page sales letter.

Sales letter - $1,100 — $4,950 + 5% commission

A well-researched, targeted long-form sales letter designed to be the point of sale. Best applied to luxury goods, tours or time shares. Usually, a 6 to 10-page letter.

Web site home page — $1,400 – $2,600

This WordPress themed page sets up the whole feel for your website. Filled with function, content and eye-grabbing appeal, this page aims at effortlessly leading your readers through your sales message. An essential component for landing your tourism business "on the international itinerary".

HospitalityCopywriting.com

Short-copy landing page — $750 - $875/page

A simple landing page for a product or offer. Often used for hotels, cosmetics, or other online businesses. The online equivalent of a trade ad: headline, a few paragraphs of descriptive product copy, and order portion.

Long-copy landing page — $1,450 - $2,250

An abbreviated version of the microsite typically used for B2B offers and products that require less description (e.g. tour package deals, promotional offers). The online equivalent of a 2 to 4-page letter.

Order device (transaction page) — $825 - $1,275

Similar to a short-copy landing page but with even less descriptive product copy; a page designed primarily as an online reply form where the visitor can either order the product or (if lead generation) request a free white paper on your investment opportunity.

Microsite — $2,250 - $4,900

A long-copy dedicated web site designed to sell a product - such as a resort membership, vacation package or time share - directly. The online equivalent of a 6 to 8-page sales letter.

E-newsletter set-up — $2,500

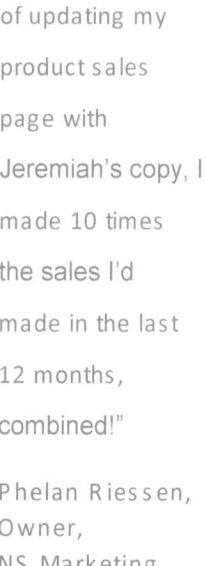

"In the first month and a half of updating my product sales page with Jeremiah's copy, I made 10 times the sales I'd made in the last 12 months, combined!"

Phelan Riessen, Owner, NS Marketing.

The process of defining your business' voice, area of expertise, outlining the newsletter's monthly sections, sending out opt-in lead e-mails to your house list, and setting up the technical side of your mail service.

Monthly e-newsletter publishing — $650

As a soft sell, 80% of each issue consists of useful information to your readership, in a likeable and expert tone with only 20% focusing on sales or promotional features. It's sharable, with social media buttons and forwarding features, and also links through to your website's archives. This is the email equivalent of a 2 to 2 ½-page blog post.

Online ad — $400 - $600

A 100-word classified ad to run in an e-zine and drive readers to a microsite or landing page.

Google AdWords placement — $225 - $300 A, B, C tests

The placement and testing of short, key word-researched headlines within target areas, demographics and languages.

Long-copy email — $1,800 - $2,400 + 5% commission

An e-mail in response to an inquiry, designed to sell a product directly by driving the recipient to a landing page. The online equivalent of a 3 to 4-page sales letter.

Teaser e-mail — $1,075 - $1,600 + 5¢ per click

A short e-mail designed to drive the readers to a microsite or long-copy landing page where they can order your product or make a reservation. The online equivalent of a ½ to 2-page sales letter.

Lead-generation e-mail — 10 mails for $1,000 - $1,400

Similar to a teaser email, but with the purpose of driving you readers to a landing page or transaction page where they can request more information before making a purchase.

Online e-mail conversion series — $1,000 - $1,400

A series of follow-up e-mail messages sent via auto-responder, designed to convert an inquiry into a reservation for your hotel/tour or sale of your product.

Direct mail package – mail order — $4,750 - $6,300 + 5¢ per mailing

A package consisting of a main sales letter, personalized "lift note", mini- advertisement "Buck slip", an order device / reply card, all designed to sell a product or vacation package.

Side-by-side ad package, house list — $1,400 – $3,500 + 5¢ per mailing

A promotion specifically tailored to groups our tourism councils that are interested in attracting attention to a city area rather than focusing on any specific business or service. Up to 10 businesses can be highlighted in this 4-6 page sales letter.

Membership renewal series — $1,250 - $2,000 / letter

Used by clubs and hotels, this 2 to 3-page sales letter offers a premium to encourage repeat patronage.

Self-Mailer — $1,750 - $3,850

A self-mailer is any promotional piece that does not require an envelope. This is often used as marketing collateral at the front desk of hotels and stores, as well as for trade shows.

Print ads — $750 - $2,500

Development of an ad to be placed in a magazine or trade journal with a strong headline, lead, proof and call to action.

Newsletters — $400 - $1,000 / 1-3 pages

Promotions that showcase specific developments of a company or industry while offing actionable advice, best practices or lessons learned. Newsletters are also used as a launching pad for company initiatives and branding efforts.

White paper – $3,000 - $3,700

This is the perfect blend between a magazine article and a brochure. With this, you demonstrate your deep understanding of your prospect's problems or desires, show how other options in the industry fail to achieve the results that they need – and highlight the fact that you can. This is also a very important weapon in any large scale bidding process. By setting the buying criteria early on, your company can effectively hold all other competitors to your high level of deliverables.

Case Study - $1,500 - $1,750

Studies show that case studies are the most important sales tools in the B2B world for producing quality leads. Not only do they demonstrate your track record and credibility, they provide a real example of proof behind your claims. The only thing that's left in the sales process then is the final push – to close.

SEO-friendly articles — $850 - $1,000

These are used to increase the value and search engine relevance of websites. While mostly informational, content must still have a persuasive call to action that involves your company's core product or area of service.

Japanese / Spanish / Chinese SEO Meta text — $150 / page

Even though your page doesn't contain any text in Japanese or Spanish, this keyword-rich meta description in Japanese and/or Spanish sends your search results right to the top. This benefits international customers who can read English but generally plan their vacations online using their native language.

Japanese / Spanish / Chinese translation services — $75 - $150 / page

Native level translations of your website's landing pages, order device, SEO articles or online ads. These are especially useful with international tour programs or mail order products such as cosmetics.

Japanese / Spanish / Chinese lead generation tweets (10) — $200 - $275

Used to create external links to your site, tweets are personalized versions of headlines, the central promise of your product, service or location and key benefits of your business.

Copy critique — $280 - $840

This is ideal for clients who want a "second opinion" on a piece of copy, or who need new ideas to inject life into an existing package that's no longer working. This is a 1-2-page executive summary.

 HospitalityCopywriting.com

FAQs regarding pricing

How do you handle payment?

- 50% of the fees are due upfront. After that, 25% is due at a mid-point which we agree on. And then, 25% is due upon completion. Copy critique fees are due 100%, upfront. And for e-newsletters, I ask for 3 months in advance.

What guarantee do you offer?

- I provide a 100% satisfaction guarantee. If you are unhappy with the work that I've done, for any reason, just let me know and I will revise the work up to 2 times within 30 days of the deadline in order to guarantee that you have exactly what you want.

What do these prices include?

- They cover: all of the research, 3 possible leads that you can choose from, the drafting process, presentation and approval, further editing, polishing, testing, revisions and, finally, your approval and / or up to 2 additional revisions (as long as they don't change the scope of the project and are assigned within 30 days of receipt of copy).
- Also, after I've completed your first package, if you are interested in doing an A/B split test - I offer a second package deal at 50% off the original price.

How do I hire you? What steps do we take?

- I have a very simple contract which explains all of the terms and expectations of my work, which I'll e-mail with my project prospectus. You can either sign it using DocuSign, or print it out and send it back to me. Then, as soon as I receive it, I'll begin work on your project right away.

What's the best way to reach you?

- Drop me a line at jeremiah@hospitalitycopywriting.com I'll give you a detailed answer to any question you may have within one business day.

I have a tight deadline. Can you get started right away?

- Due to specific scheduling demands, I can't guarantee that every service listed on my pricing sheet is available at all times. However, after speaking with you and preparing a prospectus, I am certain that I will meet whatever deadline we agree upon.

Do you charge more for rush jobs?

"Jeremiah is an amazing Idea Man. We are joint Goldmine Group members -- a group which Jeremiah founded. I've been amazed at the number of actionable ideas Jeremiah has contributed during weekly discussions. His support, enthusiasm, and ideas are most appreciated. If you're looking for someone to help move your business messaging forward, I highly recommend Jeremiah."

Nancy Ross Brewer,

Copywriter and former VISA Executive.

HospitalityCopywriting.com

o I don't do rush jobs for several reasons. Mainly, I know that if I'm not giving you a superior sales tool that will directly improve your bottom line, a rush job won't be doing either of us a favor. Just as my guarantee states – if you're not succeeding then I'm not succeeding. So, if you have a pressing deadline approaching, give me a call right away... before another day goes by, and I'll give you a clear yes or no on your project.

Additional terms?

o A signed agreement (provided by HospitalityCopywriting.com) is required for all jobs.
o Copywriting of major new tests and versions of a website is quoted separately.

"Not only did Jeremiah's email marketing campaign have 36 – 48% open rates, the quality of the content helped grow my reputation among investors, prospects and create conversations."

Jen Flynn,

Land Banking Representative, Velur Enterises

Clients and Professional Experience Page

Berlitz – A worldwide provider of high quality English as a second language education

California Sessions – Owner, food vending business in Tokyo

Café 1134 – Various art exhibitions

Café Ivy – Music performances

Café Thomas Paine – Art exhibitions

Censured Sentient – Clothing design

Chez Loma – Art exhibitions

Club Milk – Art exhibition

Coronado Art Gallery – Sales of local artists and framing

Coronado Hardware – Sales and construction

COSA School of art. – Teaching painting, photography and portfolio presentation

Createspace.com – Self-published novel, "The Mechanics of Deceit"

Denis Leudman – High-end architectural fabrication

Dr. Acevado, Eaton and Magone – Medical office

Eekokochi – Founding partner, Combination gallery, café and multi-use space

Faster Hot Water – B2B website, email marketing and direct mail

Fukunaka Kazuo – Photography book editing

G.K.A. – English instruction

Guest Centric – Partnership for Japanese and Chinese language websites, brochure

Hospitality Copwriting   Hospitality B2B copywriting services

Imagine tours – A study abroad program at a San Diego ranch

Iwasaki Genki – Translation partner

Itozaki Kimio – Artist statement development

Keating Dental Arts – Geo-centric landing pages

"A mature individual, Jeremiah is always looking to improve himself. He possesses a calm independence and a work ethic that enables him to work well with a team or individually. He is an unselfish, modest and creative individual, and I have thoroughly enjoyed working with him."

Ashley Grainger, Shinjuku Berlitz instructional supervisor.

HospitalityCopywriting.com

Koenji school of dental technology – English instruction

Loan Libre – Blog articles

Moderno – Collaborations on various book projects

Morimura Yasumasa – Editing for artists statement

Nagone Mitsuko – Artist "methodologies" statement

Nakamura Ayako – Artist statement

National Title Company – Blog articles

Northwest Point Resort – Web copy and lead generation

Nishi-Shinjuku art gallery – Art exhibition

Nova – English Instruction

NS Marketing – long-form landing page

One-Fifty-One – Team rider

Okuma Toshiyuki – Editing and English translation

OurPact – Features web copy

Owada Ryo – Artist statement, editing

PacRim Marketing – Japanese marketing collaboration

Photo Icon – Owner, photo printing and art gallery

Power Digital Marketing – Webpages and online content

Prope.com – Voice actor for "Real Ski Jump", "Real Animals" and "Power of coin"

Revolution Magazine – Promotions and booking for nationwide DJ tour

San Diego Fly Rides – Blog articles

ShinSuiSha publishers – Editing, native check and art commentary

Soccerloco – Blogging and category pages

$pleger – Bait piece

Student Loan Services – Blog articles

Subciety – Brand messaging/ design

Suspereal clothing – Art and concept collaboration

The Bay Hill Tavern – Music events

The Blasthaus – Gallery assistant

The Del Mar Law Group – Blog articles

Authored and co-authored books:

The Dot-to-Dot program – Volunteer art teacher in Mexico

The Goldmine Group – Founder, copywriting circle

The Hexagon – A copywriting circle

The Marketing Connect – Owner, marketing opportunities for tourism businesses

The Sunset Marquis hotel – Japanese social media marketing

The Rack Room – An art storage facility

The Steven Clayton Art Gallery – Sales and framing of internationally known artists

The San Francisco Museum of Modern Art – Sol Lewitt exhibition

collaboration ──────────────────────────▶

The San Diego – Yokohama Sister City Society – Board member, hotel

internship creation program

Think Reservations – web copy

Tom's language school – English instruction

Unhinge Hardware – Blog articles and category pages

University of Northern Iowa "Camp adventure" – Teenage sports camp in

Germany

Wyndham Peachtree Hotel & Conference Center – Web copy and social media marketing

Velur – Japanese landing page, email and social media marketing

All of this experience has given me one fundamental advantage as a copywriter – the ability to understand a variety of people, relationships and cultures. I believe it's this skill that helps me reach out to your audience, whoever they may be, in a very personal way and speak to them in a voice that is instantly recognizable and familiar. That's how I can show your readers that your products and services are really meant for them. That's how my promotions help you build trust, respect and repeat business.

HospitalityCopywriting.com

Samples Page

Webpages

APP website

B2C website

10 X more sales in the first month and a half than the last 12 months, combined.

B2B website

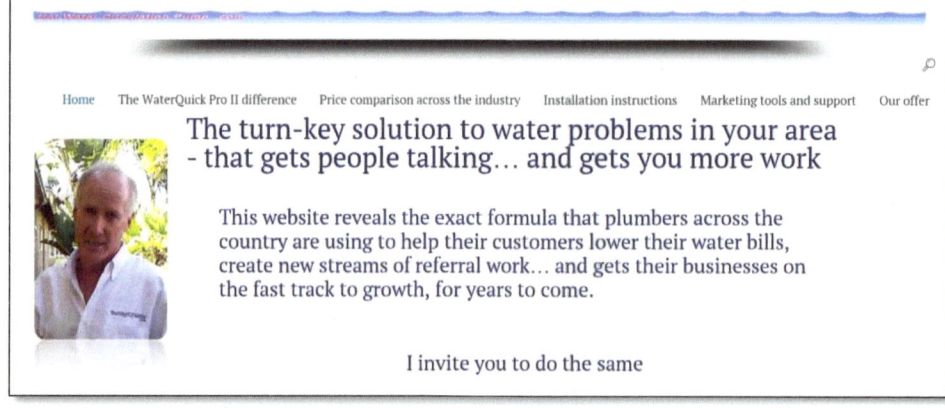

Video Sales letter and Video Blog

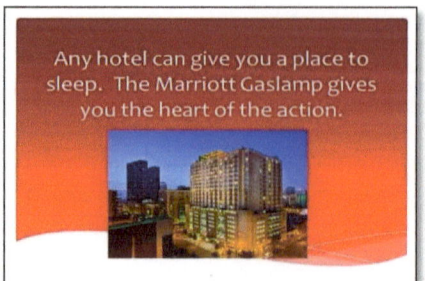

[Business proposal for financial education](#)

Your child's financial independence
– the key to bringing your family together.

[Auto-responder series for Japanese customers](#)

Email for 1 time visitors

Dear _ex. John Smith-Sama (You can use "customer" if you don't know the person's name)
Thank you for (**A**. visiting our store. **B**. staying at our hotel, **C**. enjoying our park, **D**. enjoying a beautiful evening at our venue, **E**. dining with us). We're getting more and more Japanese visitors these days and, to show our appreciation, we would like to give you a %%%off coupon for your next visit. If you post this coupon code through your social media, we will even double its value the next time you come in our doors. Just share your experience at our (**A**. store, **B**. hotel, **C**. park, **D**. venue, **E**. restaurant) friends, and show us that post the next time we see you. We're looking forward to serving you again!
Sincerely,

[Land Banking lead generation letter](#)

Why so many average Japanese office workers are quietly investing in "The California Countdown to 2020"…

Let us show you what they're so excited about… why this investment is set to take off… and how you can use the very same strategy to retire in comfort in the next 7 – 10 years.

First page ranking for the term "land banking", in Japanese

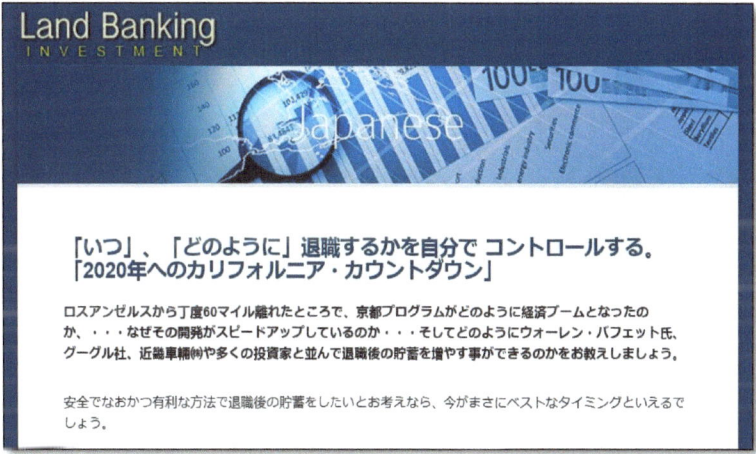

[Online interactive tourist map](#)

Land Banking Email Marketing results for 3 different prospect lists, with a $24 - $36K+ product

List	Subscribers	Opens	Clicks
List C	21	42.9%	0.0%
List A	143	43.4%	0.0%
List B	17	58.0%	5.9%
List C	21	23.8%	0.0%
List B	17	41.2%	0.0%
List C	23	33.3%	0.0%
List B	17	58.0%	0.0%
List B	17	47.1%	0.0%
List B	18	50.0%	5.6%
List A	143	36.4%	1.4%
List B	18	55.6%	0.0%
List A	144	36.8%	0.0%
List B	18	44.4%	0.0%
List A	146	36.1%	6.9%
List A	148	34.2%	0.0%
List A	148	39.0%	0.0%
List A	149	30.6%	0.0%
List A	150	36.5%	0.0%

#1 "Don't gamble with your retirement savings."

#2 "How to buy low and sell high."

#3 "An investment with more growth potential... and less stress...

#4 "The 3"S"-Strategy for avoiding another 2008 meltdown."

#5 "The myth of the rich and powerful: Debunked."

#6 "Showtime features Lancaster's solar revolution."

#7 "What investments mean to relationships."

#8 "I admit I was skeptical too..."

Travel Incentive Program

Travel Industry Interviews

Travel Tech Newsletter

24

HospitalityCopywriting.com

Special report

Over 250 Opt-ins through LinkedIn

LinkedIn article

Fundraising system info premium

Travel website info premium for lead generation

HospitalityCopywriting.com

Water Saving technology every door direct promotion

White paper -

How to raise your ADR over the next 3 years
Why 50 out of 55 markets are now above 2007 revenue PEAK...
even while the economy is still recovering...
and how you can use this opportunity to secure your long-term growth.

Monthly e-newsletter – Financial Futures

30-Day Marketing Guide for Hotels - MoreDirectBooking.com

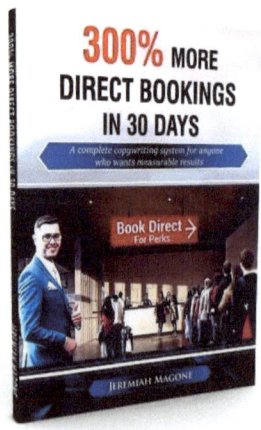

26

Writing technique page

Not many copywriters out there have received the high level of professional training provided by American Writers & Artists International (AWAI), yet this distinction is one thing that many of the most successful have in common.

Why?

- We understand "The Four Legged Stool" – a test to determine if your promotion has the Idea, Benefits, Track Record and Credibility it takes to become a successful promotion. Forget one of these and, just like a broken stool, your efforts are on shaky ground.
- We put "The 4 "U"s" into every headline and sub-head we write. This is especially crucial in our modern era of online marketing, because without quickly communicating your promotion's Urgency, Useful promise, Unique qualities and Ultra-specific information within the first few seconds, chances are that your campaign will just look like spam.
- We understand "The Law of Transparency", something which most commercials completely miss. However, just as an example of the ones that get it, look at car commercials. Think of the feelings that they evoke. That's good copy, because they aren't trying to sell the car itself. Successful copywriters will aim to sell the transformation the product bring to your life. After all, that's the core emotion that your customers are really looking for. Which means, if you want to really get your prospects' hearts racing, then your promotions had better understand this distinction as well.
- We study "The Architecture of Persuasion" day in and day out. Just as every movie has an emotional structure, tying each scene together and building the momentum to a crescendo, so does every successful sales letter. In fact, AWAI's 586 page program is dedicated to guiding copywriters through every step of that persuasion along the way. This is how I've gained all the research tools and proven formulas I need to reach out and grab your prospects by the lapel.

Just think about the explosive effect that any one of these proven techniques could have on your sales.

Now ask yourself – why would you want to run your next promotion without them?

HospitalityCopywriting.com

Many of these techniques that I mentioned above were, in fact, pioneered by <u>members of AWAI's board of directors</u>.

<u>These include:</u>

Bill Bonner - the founder and president of Agora Publishing, one of the world's most successful consumer newsletter publishers.

Bob Bly – an independent copywriter, consultant, and author of more than 70 books on copywriting and marketing.

Dan Kennedy - a copywriter for the past 30 years and one of the highest paid copywriters in the world.

Heather Lloyd-Martin - expert in SEO copywriting and considered one of the original pioneers in the industry.

Nick Usborne - online copywriter, author, and site optimization expert with over 25 years in the marketing industry.

Joshua Boswell - an online copywriting expert and secret weapon technology companies turn to for marketing success.

Mark Ford - has been directly involved in the generation of over one billions dollars of sales through the mail and online.

Rebecca Matter - Co-Managing Partner of AWAI and marketer with over 15 years of direct-response experience.

Paul Hollingshead - Co-Founder of AWAI, Paul leads a truly transformed life as one of today's most sought-after copywriters.

Katie Yeakle - Co-Founder and Executive Director of AWAI with over 20 years of direct marketing and publishing experience.

And many others...

HospitalityCopywriting.com

Take advantage of AWAI's years of fine tuning

By studying these "Greats" day after day, I've learned to write in a style that's friendly, exciting and gets results. That's because AWAI has shown me how to keep your promotions from ever being confusing, unbelievable, boring or awkward… and how to make the benefits of your products or services as vivid as possible. That's what makes AWAI different. And that's the huge advantage their insights can bring to your campaign.

Get in touch with me today and let me show you, first hand, the amazing results that high impact copy can have on your bottom line.

What others are saying about AWAI

"A Copywriting Formula That's Proven Successful"
– Carline Anglade-Cole, Million-Dollar Copywriter, and copywriter chosen to promote Oprah's latest book

"Stars in the Copywriting World Have All Come from the AWAI Program"
Chris Marlow, The Copywriter's Coach

"I've Been Working With AWAI Copywriters for Eight Years Now. They Consistently Produce Direct Mail Winners for Me"
Deeba Jafri, Marketing Consultant

"Without Good Copywriters, We Don't Have a Business. When I'm Contacted By Someone Who Has Completed AWAI's Program, Believe Me, I Always Take Their Call."
Julia Guth, Executive Director of The Oxford Club

In Fact, Our Most Successful Promo Right Now Was Written By An AWAI-Trained Copywriter … And We're Grateful."
Jennifer Stevens, Copywriter and Copy Chief for International Living

HospitalityCopywriting.com

Getting to know Jeremiah Magone

I've lived all over.

When my mother was studying to become a Doctor, we lived in a lot of different places across the country. Montana, Colorado, Seattle, Connecticut and finally San Diego. But that was just the beginning. I continued to travel on my own; living in Germany, Spain, Mexico, San Francisco, Japan, and just recently, returning to San Diego. I believe my experience traveling has given me one unique quality – the ability to understand and adjust to a multitude of cultures and attitudes. Nowhere is that skill more useful than when tailoring the voice of your promotion to really connect with your target audience.

I love a challenge.

From sport climbing to starting new businesses in America and Japan, I love to make something happen. That's why, for me, copywriting is such an interesting field to work in. I'm constantly learning new things, taking strategic steps to reach my goals and, most importantly, finishing what I start. There are always new opportunities out there; the important thing is what you do with the ones you've taken.

Doing business in Japan has changed my perspective.

For me, Japan was an MBA crash course in problem solving and networking. There, I was surrounded by friends who were business owners and high level professionals. They taught me so much by example. I absorbed their long term plans for business growth, the way that they used their buying power to leverage their market position and also, how they dealt with the downturn in business after 2008. Looking back now, I know that I was very fortunate. Japan has given me a lot... a great sense of responsibility and commitment when it comes to business, the thoroughness that's needed to maintain customer relationships, the patience to go with one approach until it really works and the judgment to adapt when it doesn't. These lessons mean that, when you work with me, I can almost guarantee that it won't feel like you've hired a freelancer – because I know that to really build lasting relationships, we all have to succeed as one.

I've learned so much by being a teacher.

In my 8 years in Japan, I had the opportunity to learn a completely new form of teaching. These are the techniques and methods that have empowered an entire multi-million-dollar industry of English education to meet the demands of a growing international market.

I can use these same techniques in your business as well. For example, if you need me to make a presentation to inform or gather input from your team – no sweat. I've done that thousands of times. Just give me a call and leave it to me. Public speaking is something I love.

Get in touch with Hospitality Copywriting right away

As a freelance copywriter, realize, it only takes 2 or 3 clients to fill up my schedule for months at a time. That means that, if you want to have your project done well, done fast and done within budget – you'll be doing yourself a favor by getting in touch with me early on, so I can have plenty of time to work up the best-selling arguments possible.

Give me a call today to talk about your project.

Sincerely,

Jeremiah Magone

Consulting Copywriter

HospitalityCopywriting.com

How to Get More Leads and Close More Contracts with your Website

Have you ever met someone who couldn't stop talking about their company's products at a party?

It's pretty annoying because it's obvious that they're trying to sell you something, right?

Unfortunately, many B2B websites still suffer from this same compulsion.

They go on and on, boasting about their product' and service' features, just like a brochure.

They inform rather than inspire.

Yet no matter how much they push, they aren't making the sale. Because just like at a party – they're steadily pushing people away.

This kills lead generation. Which in turn makes it impossible for businesses to stay in front of their target audience.

According to the National Sales Executive Association, this means they may be missing up to 80% of their real sales opportunities. No wonder so many businesses are dismayed by their website's performance.

That's why I've come up with 8, simple steps you can walk through to determine if your website is missing these important sales flash points as well. And you'll also get a few pointers in the right direction if you've happen to make any of these common mistakes.

I hope you find this guide helpful.

All the best,

Jeremiah

Jeremiah Magone

Consulting Copywriter

HospitalityCopywriting.com

This page left blank for formatting purposes

HospitalityCopywriting.com

Do you have a clear headline?

1

It fails if:

It passes if:

You clearly communicate what your site is all about with a visitor-centric unique value proposition.

People's first reaction to your headline is, "Huh?" This often happens when headlines are trying to be clever, cute or grandiose. Also, avoid using the word "Experience". Done-to-death headlines are a big red flag for visitors.

Your headline makes a promise, speaks to a problem, has a unique take on a common perception or underlines the importance of urgency. Also remember, because headlines are so important, make sure to use social media to test them!

Is your website trustworthy?

2

It fails if:

It passes if:

You clearly demonstrate that there are real people behind your website, and if your visitors send you questions, you'll get back to them immediately.

You send little signals that you aren't active on your website. This includes stale blog content, no social media feeds, no connection to the news of the day or an All Rights Reserved footer from 2014.

There are 3rd-party stickers on the top of your website to reassure your visitors. You show that you're just a phone call away. And you introduce yourself so people know they aren't just dealing with a faceless company.

close **more** contracts

HospitalityCopywriting.com

You quickly answer readers' "Oh yeah? What's that about" curiosity, when they first read your headline with a crisp, clear explanation that any 5-year old would understand.

You start describing what your company is "all about." The text takes off on a different subject from the headline. It doesn't entice the reader to spend time on your website. It bores or it doesn't point to the next logical step.

Your first few sentences are no more than 7 words long. You expand on the promise or statement in the headline to bring it into focus in a reader-benefit oriented way. And by doing this, your visitors know exactly what to expect of your site.

80% of your visitors can find exactly what they're looking for in the first 7 seconds on your site, simply by scanning.

The links are mainly at the end of sentences with words like, "Click here," or, "Learn more." You offer a Chinese menu of links instead of grouping them into logical categories. Your page flow isn't arranged according to the sales cycle.

Your 3 most important links are prominently displayed. Visitors don't have to read much to figure out where the link goes. You've included click-forward links at the bottom of each page. You use active verbs in your descriptions.

Is your copy reader-centric?

5

It fails if:

It passes if:

You answer visitors' doubts about your track record, credibility, main promise and price superiority and/or guarantee without talking about yourself. You do this by focusing on the benefit from your customers' point of view.

You find yourself starting each sentence with, "We" or, "Our". To fix this, simply put the benefit first. Instead of, "Our chefs are the best around…" Change it to: "You'll enjoy the best food around. Our award winning chefs make sure…"

Your copy always answers the 3"W"s. Why you? Why true? Why now? And the way those answers are presented keeps visitors moving forward through your sales cycle. You add momentum with active verbs, rich media and testimonials.

Do you actively guide visitors?

6

It fails if:

It passes if:

You create momentum by telling people what to do. And you keep them engaged by always promising something exciting/ useful/ informative around the corner.

You talk "about" things people will experience with your products or services but you never give them a way to actually see for themselves through a media-rich experience. Basically, your site resembles a brochure instead of a portal.

You are always showing people the next action they can take to 'get to the good stuff'. People are able to find exactly what they want with the minimal number of clicks and they always understand "what comes next" on the path to purchase.

HospitalityCopywriting.com

You offer something of exceptional value to your target audience in exchange for their email addresses. You do this while making sure they know you're secure and you're going to send something of value.

You tell them to: "sign up for news... or special offers," and you don't have anything to tell them about immediately. You find you aren't able to deliver your emails because they don't have a real reason to whitelist your address.

You have put together a special report that speaks directly to the needs, wants and desires of your target audience. As a follow up, you then start sending content that engages your audience and helps segment your list.

You're quick to respond to new sign-ups and you let them know exactly how often they'll hear from you, while giving them a taste of what to expect. After that, you work hard to build a solid 'know, like, trust' relationship.

Your communications are purely offer- or event-driven. You haven't introduced yourself, your 'tribe', or invited prospects to connect via social media. You haven't teased your next email or asked for their opinion on topics of common

You show commonality with your readers by giving them the most targeted, useful information possible. You don't include promotions or calls to action in any of the first 3 emails. After that you follow the 90% content: 10% sales message ratio.

SALES STATISTICS

48% OF SALES PEOPLE NEVER FOLLOW UP WITH A PROSPECT
25% OF SALES PEOPLE MAKE A SECOND CONTACT AND STOP
12% OF SALES PEOPLE ONLY MAKE THREE CONTACTS AND STOP
ONLY 10% OF SALES PEOPLE MAKE MORE THAN THREE CONTACTS
2% OF SALES ARE MADE ON THE FIRST CONTACT
3% OF SALES ARE MADE ON THE SECOND CONTACT
5% OF SALES ARE MADE ON THE THIRD CONTACT
10% OF SALES ARE MADE ON THE FORTH CONTACT
80% OF SALES ARE MADE ON THE FIFTH TO TWELFTH CONTACT

Source: National Sales Executive Association

(If your website isn't following up, even once, what chance do you have, really?)

With the majority of hospitality business coming through online channels these days, it only makes sense to have the most engaging website possible.

It's not a catalogue with nice pictures and descriptions, it's a hub of communication, a portal of discovery… and thanks to the automation that technology offers… it's a major revenue channel working for you, 24/7! So then, why do so many businesses *still* treat it like a parking space for old sales brochures!

I'd love to add your website to the list of positive examples to point to when people want to optimize their websites. Please get in touch, share a few of your best practices and I'll be sure to highlight your site in the next version of this guide.

- Jeremiah

Key Copy Platform

This Key Copy Platform outlines all the elements of OurPact's branding message. Please note, this is not complete for privacy reasons. A complete document also includes competitor research, market trends, and future obstacles/ action plans.

✓ Business tag line:
- **"It's just thoughtful parenting"**
- By using <u>quotes</u> we show that this is something one parent would say to another (while they're recommending OurPact)
- The word '<u>parenting</u>' is the goal of our prospects because currently they feel out of control.
- By using the word '<u>thoughtful</u>' we make people stop and think, "why thoughtful"? The answer. We all want our children to look back and think of us as "thoughtful parents" one day, even when we didn't always have time to be there for them 100%. This is a way of subtly promising that they will.
- By using the words '<u>It's just</u>', it's obvious we're telling someone about something that sounds complicated but it's really simple.
- This headline is:
- A. Useful – It's something that will show me how to be a thoughtful parent
- B. Unique – I've heard "smart parenting" before, but never "thoughtful parenting". As such, it must be talking about something new and unique.
- C. Urgent – The topic of parenting is always urgent because of constantly evolving worries.
- This headline isn't:
- C. Ultra-specific – We don't know what "It" is. However, this mystery lets us use this quote in a lot of different situations with the parent playing the 'hero' because of their thought and consideration for their children.

✓ Social and psychographics description of your specific target market:
- 65% of prospects are stay at home and working mothers who are tired of their children's addictive mobile device habits. They feel bad that they've allowed their children to become so needy for constant entertainment. But now that it's become a way of life, they have no idea how to get their kids to "put down the iPad and come to dinner!"

39

- 35% of prospects are fathers who fall into 2 categories. 60% are just as unhappy about the lack of family time over the dinner table as their wives. 40% feel that too much mobile device use has led to an inactive lifestyle and weight gain.
- 60% of all prospects feel that too much mobile usage leads to introverted behavior. 40% are worried about their children's health because of staying up late. 30% are afraid of cyber-bullying issues. 25% are concerned about inappropriate content.
- 96% of all people feel this is a problem but very few have any idea of what to do about it.

✓ An explanation of the real human value of your business' products and services
- This app gives parents a way to finally talk to their children about the right and the wrong place of technology in their children's lives. But they won't just preach, because their children will actually listen.
  Why? This app enforces set schedules on each individual device. Therefore, within a few days, children learn that they have to be good in order to gain more time. This means they have to talk with their parents in order to work out mobile device schedules that are best for everyone. This leads them to be more communicative and, ultimately, more aware of their schedules. This leads to responsibility. Ultimately, parents will feel happy knowing that they're doing something to keep their children from falling into addictive behavior. And children will be able to enjoy more in life because they won't be spending 50 hours a week glued to their mobile devices.

✓ A unique selling proposition statement:
- OurPact is the only parental control app capable of blocking all app and internet access. This makes it easy for you to set limits on how much time your children are spending on their mobile device apps and social media... so you can bring balance back to your family time.

✓ Your emotional selling position. These are statements tied to core emotional benefits. AKA – buying buttons
- By having control, OurPact helps you talk with your kids about the important issues in their lives, and that guides them to become more successful adults.
- Bring the family dinner back to life
- Provide motivation for chores and homework
- Have better communication
- Create balance – Stay connected
- Encourage communication and compromise
- With OurPact, you can restore balance

- ✓ Product positioning statement. This shows how you want your business to be perceived in the market
  - It's not about control. It's about working together so everybody wins. It's just thoughtful parenting.

- ✓ Testimonials, expert and celebrity quotes along with mentions in popular media
  - Below. There are basically 5 types of testimonials.
    1. I'm so glad that my kids finally listen to me – no more fights for the iPad!
    2. You've helped improve the quality of our family time
    3. My kids finally have a healthy schedule again
    4. This has helped my family talk about the good and bad points of tech.
    5. This helps me stay connected to what my kids are doing and that helps me keep them out of trouble. Bullying, explicit content, etc…
  - Negative comments: The app doesn't have as many finite controls. When the 'app/ internet blocking time' is over, the phone icons don't return to their original positions. This causes children to complain.

- ✓ Key message benefit statements with well-researched facts to support your main selling points
  - Creating schedules is the quickest and easiest way to restore balance to your children's mobile device habits.
  - On average, kids are spending up to 55 hours a week with their eyes glued to their mobile devices, according to the American Academy of Pediatrics.
  - This addictive behavior has been show to lead to:
    1. Introverted behavior
    2. Lack of personality development
    3. Physical, mental and emotional problems
  - Competing products are inferior for 3 reasons:
    1. They are a $16 a month. OurPact is free.
    2. They don't block app use. Kids use their phones to play apps 60% of the time. OurPact is the only app powerful enough to block apps.
    3. They offer too many controls and so they're harder for parents to start using immediately.

- ✓ Key message benefit statements designed to overcome anticipated objections

HospitalityCopywriting.com

- You'll be surprised by how fast your kids will stop complaining about the fact that you 'locked' their phones, and start talking with you about what they can do to earn a little extra time. Homework, chores, get to the dinner table on time... Check. Check. Check.

✓ A list of essential headline elements and samples to include in your marketing pieces

- Show that this app isn't about controlling your children. It's about making choices together.
- Tell parents to fill their kids 'bucket list' – Give your children more memorable experiences in life by showing them how to put their phones away and simply enjoying the time together.
- It's about creating more conversations by showing kids how to "put it down" and enjoy connecting with friends and family.
- Remind parents that even if their kids complain at first... this might be the first time that they've been able to have "the tech talk" with your kids. We think that's definitely a step in the right direction.

--Testimonials--

Family Dinners are Back

I'm a father of two, and cell phones at dinner had become a big problem in my family. I used the app last night and was surprised how quick and easy it was to set up and how effective it is. Thank you for reviving our family dinners. A job well done.

- MrSamson007 – Feb 5, 2015

Parental Responsibility, Yes Indeed...

Love this App. I knew my kids were spending too much time on their devices. After a while, I frankly got tired of shouting, "Turn it off." Now, I can fulfill my RESPONSIBILITY as a parent by having my kids on a much needed schedule. After one week, your kids will get used to it like mine have & actually become more responsible young adults. I love it. Thank you!

- Benny& the kids – Feb 13th, 2015

Helping Parents Manage Screen Time

I LOVE this app because it manages my children's screen time for me. No more yelling or asking a million times to turn off the tablet. I simply set a schedule for each of my children and the app takes care of the rest! I even use it to make sure I don't get too much screen time too!

-Spazymunky – February 16th, 2015

Remote Control!

These days somehow the biggest threat to our kids, in terms of disciplining them, has become losing use of their iPads. Unfortunately, they still find their way to them before we realize it. The typical answer is that they "forgot" they couldn't use their IPad during the school week or "I just had to check one thing". Now excuses don't work because their iPads don't – when we don't want them to. The remote control function is wonderful. Whether at work or on the road I can grant or deny use.

-Modern day parent – Feb 6, 2015

OurPact Simply Works!   ★★★★★

OurPact helps us reign in our child when he needs to be. Very easy to use and to schedule when the iPhone can & cannot be used. Period! Thanks!

-Cyrus M., March 8th, 2015

HospitalityCopywriting.com

Focus!

Incredibly useful. Allows me to grant or deny my son access to his iPhone so he learns to use it as a tool instead of a toy. Prevents him from getting distracted while doing his school work. Thumbs up!

-George4960 – Feb 4th, 2015

Genius

Now when I say, "Stop – put it away," they know I mean it! Genius!

-Margo & Kids – Feb 5th, 2015

Curving positive online behavior

WOW! So impressed with this app. If you are a parent this is a MUST. I love how they are all about having parents work together with their children as a unit to curve positive online behavior. If you are looking for an easy, fast, and effective mobile parental control app – it has finally arrived.

- Roush333 – Feb 5th, 2015

Get Control of Family Tech Use with OurPact

With the OurPact app, I like that they keep families in mind, and allow parents to use it not just as a parental control tool but as a family guidance tool. It allows families to put schedules in place when it comes to internet and app use that are based around daily schedules, weekday and weekend uses.

-Drifterplus1 – Feb. 6th. 2015

I usually don't bother to write a review

I usually don't bother to write a review, but this app has really changed my family for the better. As a result of using this app for about a month, I feel that our family has grown closer. Even though it was designed to curb kids' device time, the grant additional time feature really helps me positively reinforce good behavior.

–Thankful2015, March 12th, 2015

HospitalityCopywriting.com

Best Parenting App by Far

I've used parental control apps in the past and this one is the best by far. The setup is easy and it doesn't slow down the Internet or phone like other parental control apps. I no longer have to worry about my kids staying up all night watching movies on their iPads

-AllenDaddy124 – Feb 5th, 2015

Definitely recommended!!

This app is amazing, I finally feel like I have control as a parent again. I want my kids to have fun playing games and communicating with their friends, but don't want them losing sleep at night because they're using their devices. This app is a lifesaver!

-SOOOOOMAD – February 4th, 2015

GREAT APP

This app does everything you want and more. No more worrying about the kids playing games all night instead of doing homework! Check this app out!

-ngst8465764398760, February 5th, 2015

At Ease, Parents

A breakthrough for new and seasoned parents in a time when our children's exposure to the media is an ever growing concern. Highly Recommended.

-YBCalDelta – Feb. 4th, 2015

OurPact is the ANSWER for any parent who loves their children

I told my relatives in the military about OurPact since they're concerned about parenting their children, but are worried about family divisions due to distance. But now, even 5000 miles away, they feel like they're close to home. They have their finger on the pulse of every situation impacting their children, whether positive or negative.

-Joe M. – Feb 5th, 2015

GREAT APP ★★★★★

In an era when the traffic of unsafe material on the internet is at an all-time high, this app sets the bar in protecting your children from inappropriate material. If you're a parent of children who are currently using the internet, this is the best app out there!

-SD Daddy – Feb. 4th, 2015

HospitalityCopywriting.com

No more battles of the iPads   

The kids now know when it's time to do homework, and go to bed without fussing. No more battles of the iPads.

-Benomgxp – March 1st, 2015

From a Tech Guy   

I highly recommend OurPact to parents with kids of any age. It's an incredibly well thought out application and user interface. The team did a great job with the build out. Cheers!

-codybarbo – Feb 6th, 2015

Wowoweewow   

This app is really great. I am a single father of two and even though I may not be there all the time, I feel like I am able to keep an eye on my kids even when I'm at work. The best part is when my kids call or text me for more time. I've never felt closer and more in control. Great work guys!

–Chuckie'sSushi – March 12th, 2015

No More Battles!   

No more battles about negotiating more time on their devices. No more battles about having to physically take their devices away from them. I am a mom of three and loved the ease of downloading this app and being able to set schedules for each child. Also LOVED being able to control their devices remotely!!! Now, if only I could get my husband off his devices…

-   NoMoreBattlesInThisHome – Feb 10,2015

HospitalityCopywriting.com